Rome That Heavenly Country

Rome That Heavenly Country

James Liddy

ARLEN HOUSE

Rome That Heavenly Country

is published in 2011 by
ARLEN HOUSE
an imprint of Arlen Publications Ltd
42 Grange Abbey Road
Baldoyle
Dublin 13
Ireland
Phone/Fax: 353 86 8207617
Email: arlenhouse@gmail.com

Distributed internationally by
SYRACUSE UNIVERSITY PRESS
621 Skytop Road, Suite 110
Syracuse, NY 13244–5290
Phone: 315–443–5534/Fax: 315–443–5545
Email: supress@syr.edu

ISBN 978–1–85132–022–6, paperback

Typesetting | Arlen House
Cover Image | Patrick Inglis Melia

CONTENTS

For Rembert Weakland
for his fidelity

"Everything in the world will pass away.
In eternity only love will remain".
– Benedict XVI, address to cardinals

"I am not afraid of the future of the Church … She will always have the last word because she has received the Divine Guarantee. No, it is for the nations of today that I tremble …"
– Pius XI, 1938

"The Pope has died. I regret his demise because I fear they will elect a new Pope who will serve the mad Duce".
– Zinaida Hippius, 10 February 1939

ROME THAT HEAVENLY COUNTRY

PRIESTS/WOMEN

"It is a great consolation that Mother's Day
and St. Monica's Feast fall on the same day.
I see some women wearing beautiful things,
I am wearing something pretty myself,
a new vestment thanks to the estate
of Elma Zilmer, her son Joe is in church.
The vestment also comes in green, violet,
and red. In the lesson St. John says 27 times
that God is love. Brothers and sisters, love?
The bad news about love is people philosophize
what it means. The good news is we know
what it is, we have memory, we look back.
The Trinity took on flesh, there is a mix
of men and women in us, so why not in God?"
(Priest at Rose's, Clintonville)

Jesus entered the place and was hemmed in
by women: Claude Ollier's brief on
Kafka, "Recognised, liked, admired,
surrounded by women".

Mary at his feet, his specialness
set her longing – Meister Eckhart's
caption, "Consolation and delight
she drew from the mouth of Jesus".

The kitchen sister got her name called twice.

A strange gold-clad animal
Media-entombed:

catch butterflies in God's mind
and stomach

God is butterfly master
and I am his estranged moth.

Ladies
baptize you bury you console you.

To Parochial Schools

I'm writing this on a Swiss-American farm
Kubly's place of course. What's important

in writing? Twilight quarries of course
cocktail questions: does Plato contain divine

jurisprudence, does the physical imagination
perform as possible melody in Your Voice?

My Lord You were in the sixties' caresses
I carry a banana tree with green fruit from there ...

A Parochial teacher did not point to the tray
Your songs are poured on or the hangouts of alibis.

A teacher will only moralize not encourage,
there's no drop of banana juice in his mouth.

My Christmas

Some evening you'll wander in
on sabbatical from my favourite star.
Trying out the affectionate words I know
I keep watching the door,

I'll be on flame then
because you'll relight my candles.

"At what time", I've been muttering
since we were introduced, "At what time ..."
I took a souvenir from your yellow
Hair – the vision that disappears so soon.
"I love you, I love you",
I can keep on repeating that.

Do you hear me, I love you;
our madness has been warming up
all these comets' years since you saw me
from your room in the stars and I you.

– from the German of Else Lasker-Schuler

The Archbishop paid three *ad limina* visits over 15 years to the Vatican with auxiliary bishop Dick Sklba. Each visit the Pope asked the same questions, "Sklba, what nationality is that? Is it Polish?" "No, Holy Father, it is Slovak". The Pope interrogated Weakland, "What age are you", the inference being obvious: is there the slightest chance you are getting close to retirement age.

Season's Compliments

L'Arbre de Noel

The tinseled tree danced tenderly with me
through the night at the Cana Club
I knew I had a high ranking one in my arms.

The tree with its Magdalene hands
performed the passing out dance and the kissing
  dance
I knew the music was alcohol I held the parade kick
of James Joyce the alto shuffle of James Stephens.

I tangoed the tree down to the basement
I kissed it I said it was more my buddy than Jesus
it was as if I met the friend I had before marriage.
Were there Christmas trees before the electric switch?
Yes the hearth was worship and cemetery of trees.

A Druid at Christmas

Our literature is or used to be the priesthood
responsible administering the religion
of our place somewhere else. I am the spokenperson
for the "country under ours", the spells and
seduction chamber music of that third estate
in spasms chorusing from standing stones, raths.

Above us Latin trembled on the balcony, the
Holy Father wore Pilate's merciful eyes which were
made of emeralds. That antiphon from Rome but I
  gaze
under it at our fading first country of poisoned wells

and rock pools, nothing but quarries, Cuchulain drives
an accelerating bulldozer past the Hill of Tara.

I play carols on the piano adorned in a collar of gold
in the music I take my ancient tree (that northern light)
remodeled to Rome and place it at the foot of the
Cross
where Vergil's shepherds provide provenance,
we're full partners in Domus Aurea's champagne.

Christmas I thought mother's not around
then there will be no real drinking.
The dead drive round in my bed-night mind
sometimes they rent cars or maybe they buy them.
My family was never righteous
they can't suffer changes of heart.
Star leads us down the valley of pines to paradise
bulbs
pining for melody and mediocrity
I like the student who is nuts about baseball
and gets the bus to the stadium
and the one who lives in the suburbs
and composes poems about his mom.
I am the mother and father of bachelor parties
and it doesn't bother me there is a mother
in Christianity and no wife.

I thought of the Christmases
before these tinseled trees
I thought of the Masses before there were Malls
I listen to Music in bed that's the night mind.

I dream at Christmas of liberation
of Abe Lincoln
(who was our first President
our first war President)
taking a brandy tastefully
signing the Proclamation.

Next morning in the class
a black man is wearing
a blue ribbon that reads
"Membership in the NAACP".

An older white woman
gamely asks, "What is
the NAACP?"
He looks intensely at her.

Jolly Vatican 2

I've had my first drink of the day, it's after Cinderella
  Hour
I've taken the cup and sang "For he's a jolly good
  fellow"
under my breath. Part of my faith is at the supper
  Jesus set up
a restaurant and bar and trained to be the bartender
  (The Church
interrupted service for a long while but it has been
  relicensed).

Divine Mercy Sunday

Though I haven't seen much of it
I warm to it, I like distant mercy.
Can you show mercy if you're close?
I feel a shadow hand arch over me,

A Voice says, "I want you to hold
my hand, I hold yours". Mercy
means the right hand at last
knows when the other one sighs.

Popcorn or bread, popcorn it is
for travellers of shiny future taverns.
They too hear a voice, "Whose sins
I have forgotten I will not mention".

Easter rings with cell phones, clue
into the arrangements. I forgive in
a martini circle, mercy has a joke,
do the olives come from the Mount?

My Bulb

If touching and moving your body is illegal
does sufficient evidence exist to convict us?
We've been arrested loitering under the tree.

Ditty

I went out on Christmas Day in the morning to the
  Mall
to purchase jigsaw puzzles and cookies for my Saviour

but, Bing, why do you send down so much white
  stuff?
Please be Our Lord the Sun call his Hollywood bluff

WHEN THE CATHOLIC CHURCH IS NOT CHRISTIAN 1

The Gospel for the 23rd Sunday in Ordinary Time,
Jesus remarks, "If anyone comes to me without hating his father
and mother, wife and children, brothers and sisters,
and even his own life, he cannot be my disciple" (*Luke* 14:25).
Wow, where does that leave the weddings the weekend?
"Holy smokes", says Fr. Carl Last, Rector of the Cathedral,
"What a message for a beautiful September day like this!"

Jesus is indeed the mediator of a renewed covenant
but at Trent, ritual: incensed vestments lights before
Saints.
You are the Princeling of a German State. Sir, do not
think
God loves you because you loot monasteries and
break saints'
statues. The question is: will you receive salvation
unless a Catholic monk under a vow of poverty listens
to remorse? Now it's calmed down. In godly
appointed
homes Deity takes the form of a replica of Martin
Luther,
on liberal near campus walls of Martin Luther King –
these are not idols people have to take down and turn
away from but they need some historical work.

When the Catholic Church is not Christian 2

Jesus was upfront on the implementation of The Social
  Question
He was a Christian
he was a Marxist
he hated the stylistics of power inserted into
  possessions
he hated literally objects people surround themselves
  with
the house the car the microwave the exercise machine
the house contents the insurance premiums of him
  and her
the car the jalopy the hot rod trotted out for show
the car for a doctor a therapist a Day Care Centre a
  soccer game
The eye of the needle the well-off their investment
brokers their Condo agents can not squeeze through
it didn't matter what shareholders thought in their
  hearts
didn't matter if they donated time as volunteers or
  activists
Jesus was an avatar at dawn he rose the morning's
lyricist the highbrow coach of escalations
Revolution was the donkey he rode on to break power
he was a pre-Lenin paladin (hammer and sickle still
  flowers)
the poor shall entertain him in heaven
The State should give citizenship papers to the soul
The State should grant free passports to beauty
for those earning less than average free Sunday
  brunch
and Cafeteria discounts on weekdays
What made the difference his speech was consecrated
what made the difference he was God we hold his
  hand

and we drink wine in the Cathedral as a preliminary
and we should tell Fr. Hammer he gets it wrong
preaching on people's faults not the social question

– *Luke* 12: 13-21

TO THE VIRGIN IN SUMMER

Brazen summers or those
where you lose your nerve
but this summer we can meet
in the bar to have some drinks
which some people call prayers.
Please read my glass as if you
were reading my palm. I am
devout and pagan maybe you
will send a recommendation
for a forthcoming reincarnation.
The soul is the formula we have
to invent the middle time and
that allows us to end in strength.
You will have to think harder
because us your Western children
stay high but not dry. On the
other hand we promise we will
not stop singing your hymns nor
leave each other. I remember
your house at Loreto I'll travel
there and sing your presence.

The Personal Interview, Folks

You bought a house or condo and all? No.
You travelled by car not public transport? No.
You argued for the death penalty didn't pray for those
on death row? No.
You were pleased by the unprofitable steward John
Paul II? No.
You were displeased by the profitable steward
Rembert Weakland? No.
You hid your talents in the ground with Vatican I
begrudgers and/or Opus Dei? No.
You didn't imagine the just war theory applied to your
country? No.
Were you prepared to receive communion if John
Kerry was denied it? No.
Was planning for retirement much on your mind? No.
You harassed your children about health benefits? No.
You played golf twice a week? No.
You didn't see friends after you married didn't see
friends if they married? No.
You didn't go to the hospital when your friend lay
dying? No.
You believed every day of your life wasn't life? No.
You went to the doctor when nothing ailed? No.
You went to Vegas? No.
You spent beer time in Sports bars? No.
You saw the *Da Vinci Code* or Mel Gibson's movie? No.
You believed marriage was for male and female? No.
You didn't see your neighbour's soul? No.
You didn't believe in the marriage of souls? No.
You hugged with your hands above the belt? No.
You sent flowers from a flower shop? No.
You weren't ready to give alms to alcoholics? No.
You thought priests' corruption was worse than that
of victims and their lawyers? No.

Did you see everything and nothing as representing
God? (Trick question, yes and no.)

Did you know Church was bartender of Sacraments
and love? Yes.
Did you understand God was outside you? Yes.
You have an idea how a teacher of righteousness
behaved on your street. Yes.
You believe The Holy Ghost is a real ghost. Yes.

(Jesus's voice in a rush, "If you deviate by more than
five from the above answers,
you cannot go onto my house immediately and find
yourself a drink").

Radio Lambeth, T.S. Eliot Speaking

A petit curse on mothers of liberal feelings who mine
them
and self help to devise guidelines for the children.
Mothers
who perform on humanistic levels do not heed
dysfunction;
may they as they wane and pain commence nibbling
at beer
to get into their skulls we live here but we are not from
here.

St. Benedict in the Cave

For Mark Tierney O.S.B.

Only the solitary are at their station
inside themselves
in remote places
identities miles from ivory tower gates
though songs fly from birds
sitting on branches magical counters of trees.
I knelt in the cave three "prison years"
the sky blanket of people in the distance
came forward like stars and moths.
I had flowerbeds at the entrance
but people didn't arrive to admire but to listen.
My gift the will of the lips:
"I can't object to you staying here
though we'll have a town and towers
you'll meet to chant and invoke the Sayer
and you'll have to bow
bowing is liturgy".
My writ in the cave made people feel hollow
the kitchen flowers spoke often
their voices quiet as Matins.
Outsiders sent me invitations
they handed me a vase of poisoned wine
which broke in pieces as I blessed it
then a poisoned loaf on a plate
I called a raven to bear it away
where it would harm no one.
The bird carried it there and flew back to me.
Flesh like you I am chosen from flesh
we are left to become flesh
in the body language of the Sayer.
In the cave I wrote words on the wall
"Who am I
maybe the guardian of commitments".

FROM THE BEACH

The ocean of love is shadowed into our
beach through (partly) the wave image of
personal relationship. When the image
is not distinguished or if you don't know

monogamy excludes God the origin of
a mistake is there. That ocean turns into
pints of water splashed out on the street
running from down pipes and gutters.

My Ps. XIII

I've taken this starry ride in
a stylish car with a few
bouts of demented anxiety.
Close to road's end let me
speak: gratitude for the ordeal
of the martyrs, admiration for
the Primacy of Rome, prayer
I travel gracefully a last lap.

Dubliners James Joyce Columba Marmion

Trees of life of knowledge
we can clarify ourselves between them,
it comes down to what you follow on the leaves
but in the foliage I watch two stars:

a man in Zurich writes his own Torah
a collection of the words God had in his barns
for the holy city of Dublin

an Abbot writes a letter to a religious
on allegory and parable and image
clairvoyant letter thrown in the morning mail.

The leaf that reads, "streets
and night ballades must not be forgotten".
The leaf that reads, "rooftop songs
can be put in a heavenly city's pulpit".

In Edermine in the mansion there's a banquet
in a room of real live monks supping from
barrels of Sir John Powers whiskey

the guests wash their hands in dream water
blessing the room by silently jesting,
the dessert arrives someone – that Marmion –
imagines the waitresses' trays at Cana.

Sentences on life sentences on knowledge
perched somewhere in the trees' bark
pages that spread their leaves now
and we decipher Irish transpiration.

In my Father's house so many observatories
the learned astronomer is in old age,
he can observe two star-like creatures
walking in dappled Stephen's Green grass.

Brother & Sister

If I could speak past
your reservation, which is
not spiritual resistance,
for a goldheart congregation
("braveheart" a desperate tribalism).
Goldheart appears in Luke,
"You must leave your father and mother –
even your wife –
brother and sister to follow me ..."

"Family" is a kind of loss?
"Leave" includes maybe a kind
of after-return?
Who speaketh the above sentence,
not Church nor Luke,
gold the soul?
Could there be a new brother and sister,
a priesthood of low tone,
modest recharging?

A Day in August a Wicked & Holy Month

First Version

An incense cloud a voice murmurs of
momentary non-social loneliness, love hides
in its snow. What lies in my brother's eyes
besides dust, in our long gaze … sunshine?

We know the prophetic message is reliable?
Because it is written, because it is insoluble and
it takes prisoners we are its prisoners, as to a
jail lamp shining. The sun's mantra takes it

slow through our mouths. Tents of embraces,
one for you Rabbi, one for Archbishop Weakland,
for us. Under this poem on stone lies Agape
remembering a tune: God, you are a nice man.

Second Version

We lie on the flat of our backs
our dreams come picture book true,
we stretch on our sides Eros or
Aphrodite hold out their hands,
I put my neck back on the pillow
gardens in each other's chest.

Skin whiter than snow works
up a manna of sweat, shoulders
shine oasis lamps, mountain
track to a golden sun, pilgrim
routes, locust swarm of heather
breaths, saliva's guitar opens
with a long big wet number.

Message made out of sound
surge here at us, "Children,
take other children more seriously,
get stuck on a few of them,
place your hands through their hair,
your mouth on their mouths,
O also buy drinks, be merry at night".

– August 6 (Transfiguration)

The Emperor Has Clothes

On the street the last one Karl wears
clothes shining like saints' vestments.

GEORG TRAKL

His eyes stood … a distance …
as a boy had already been to heaven.

That's why his words came out
on blue and white clouds.

We quarreled about religion,
but always like playmates,

and carried God from mouth to mouth.
For in the beginning was the word.

The poet's heart, a mighty fortress.
His poems: singing theses.

He was indeed Martin Luther.

His Trinity soul was in his hand
when he went into the Holy War.

I knew he had died –

His shadow requiemed mysteriously
upon the after-twilight of my room.

– from the German of Else Lasker Schüler

Cain's eyes are not beautiful to God,
Abel's face is a golden garden,
Abel's eyes are nightingales.

Abel always sings clear
with the chord-branches of his soul.
The graves of the city bisect Cain's body.

And he will murder his brother –
Abel, Abel, your blood spills into heaven.

Where is Cain, for I want to demolish him:
Cain, have you slain the song birds
in your brother's face?

– from the German of Else Lasker-Schüler

In the Cloud

I put my head in the cloud
I was touched by it
I said I must write about that cloud.

Immediately there appears the son. The father and son
  dance begins.
I know him, I don't know him.

Jesus meets and merges with the fishermen. He is not
  like "the doctors".
Still dark, he rises, leaves the house, to the open
  countryside. Before
dawn to the country light (those spaces).

He withdraws towards the sea, goes to the hills,
  through the cornfields,
the emphasis is on the disciples, having friends
  around, maybe bridegrooms.

The boat is in a storm, the waves obey, he awakes, "If
  the dead arise
from the dead the living can escape from the family.
  The Son of God is
disengaged from family, it is not quite about this.
  Think as much
about ghosts as about sex or children".

When he was walking on the water they thought he
  was a ghost.
A ghost is always coming towards us, until we are
  ghosts.

He seeks to remain unrecognised.

Garments turn into snow and words say, take up that shitty piece of wood,
as if the cross turns into a snow shower. Put black roses on the cross.

What happens? "This generation" never happens.

Jesus's promises: 100 burning houses, 100 lost brothers or distant sisters,
persecution or the persecution complex.

Jesus's commands bring up the question: seduction and conversion merge.
Perhaps we may take seduction where we can. We can't change the divine mind,
maybe we can revise it. The other query, shall we dead awaken? Get with
sacrificial persons, like Edith Stein or Berryman. I speak as an ancient Catholic
and so does Richard Rodriguez, "Catholicism, specially the Irish and Mexican
versions that shaped me, always took seriously the implications of Good Friday –
life is suffering. Whereas Protestantism seems to be centered on the Easter promise –
you can be born again".

Be practical, if arrested words will come like sleep.

The Son of Man gathers his elect. Bet they are not those who "teach like doctors".

Pretend you're not teaching, hide you're writing an essay on love …

Bet Jesus talked about art and beauty when his friend
Mary was criticised
pouring costly spikenard. Bet he thought, this is a
wonderful thing that
is happening to me.

Bet he'd hang around the Vatican Museum.

Treat yourself to being reserved, love equals
breakdown.

At the supper the couches are in place with the
glasses. The apostles drink
in part because they know they have to deal with the
horror of betrayal

(Wine in heaven, the father washes away the jeers
from his son's face).

To empty yourself of divine certitude: that kind of
drinking.

What is there? Jesus, his father and mother. What is
real? Bridegroom,
brother, sister, some form of sweetheart.

When the friends desert him, the bridegroom in a
white linen sheet shadows
him. Sunekolouthei ... Wrapped in white.

Witness; nakedness; uncertainty; memory.

First love idea is best love idea.

On his deathbed, Charles Olson, "There are holy
things, but nobody knows
they are holy".

The cup of wine in Jesus's mind.

Join hands. The church transmits this narrative. The
story in the Gospels can not
be confined to the Gospels. How many of them did
Jesus write?

There is this one.

St. Mark

My Archbishop

Though dolled up like Rome in silver and gold
bishops don't know how to hit a dance floor,
he tore the ballroom up
intensely caught in sexuality for a moment
God allowed him fire eye.
He was one of the intelligent children in the world
he recycled delight for church,
no child had done that since Newman
who was called to temporary sexual love by angels.
Trapped in a loveless marriage with his
people (evangelist that he was)
he read his office as he moved in a hurry,
not a regret that he issued decrees
for new or dazzling redone wall-iconography,
he embroidered church in a new bind.
The band stopped dancers silent
this is the silence where the Sacrament performs.
Was he the prince of a new era or was
a new prince, and he himself a bishop carried
in gold and silver through the media
doing a much better job than Polish Rome.

WEDDING POEM

I think we can avoid some of the benefits of the Enlightenment if we avoid the 18th century which was not the best 100 years for the Irish. We will have to forget the last of the bards to do that. It can be done if we can find the future plus arcady plus religion plus joy, we did that last night, helped by holy winter and its snow music coming in.

My season, this sometimes (often) comic white season means – frat boy sweetheart, email means you're always on sweetheart alert – working on two projects: fingering that energy to kiss with unboring repetition, hunting the right menus on tables. The waltzes of this climate think food over kisses. Last night we bumped in to what can be called complex enchantment, the priest blessed you in the Cuban restaurant when you had enough rum to go up to him – he worked in the parish you were married in (knew Thursday was your rehearsal night). Winter: that young big priest and you drunk in the same place.

You just married, you and I in love, six years I've been telling you I wanted a married man. Firebombing monogamy is difficult work.

From East Side Child & Youth Ministry

The story of creation the long days God put in
we are learning God is duty and fun at the same time
we have been making prayer books
Love Pat Tony Jacky Samantha Tess

We read about Adam & Eve the first temptation
we learned how to spell "Jesus" and "Church"
we have been following the paper trail they left
Love Joe Ryan Casey Kelly

We are writing a newsletter to our parents saying
what we know and what they have forgotten
we debate the priorities in the 10 Commandments
Love Jo Bob Katie Jen Mark

We know Jesus means you can get good advice
St. Valentine is a smart saint there are 3 of them
Fr. Walsh please wear black vestments at Halloween
Love Sean Emily Jeff Natalie

Extract from East Side Child & Youth Ministry Report Not Presented to the Parish

It's six weeks to Christmas and wine at Midnight Mass

LABOURERS ARE FEW

Say your commission is not to
immerse yourself in Pagan territory
by attendance at weddings of
Pagan Christians or at reunions,
dance club, casino, golf course
they talk and joke around in.

Say you have been given power
over unclean spirits translated
you are empowered as a critic
to speak and write what is not
bruited about in journal, column,
blog, writing program workshop.

Say you must be more zealous
than that and interrogate shades
of the bad and good in people
and set out your criteria in print,
a thin line in front of you between
criticism and being judgmental.

– *Matthew* 9–10

Everywhere he went people pretended they hadn't
  seen him before.
He asked, "What do you say a man is worth, is he
  divine?"
"You're a philosopher, a scientist ...?"
"You, what do you say, you've had a drink with me".
"You're the best bartender in the city".
"My flesh and blood has poured the glass for you ...
Peter, I will buy you a bar, you will be the manager,
make sure the Lutherans the mothers against drunken
  drivers find fault with you, I will stand behind you
  as you speak".
He worried about identity theft, none should say who
  he was.

– *Matthew* 16:13–20

Ask

Jesus as a psychiatrist knew how to play demons.
Not the point.
The Gospels are not reality TV.
they're partly
the teaching stories of the early Church.
Jesus can be the Rabbi
of severity, it's a teacher's ploy.
My students say, "Are you testing me?"
"I test you when I feel like it".
The woman had spunk, attitude, the hard soft thing.
Ask and the demon departs.

If I was a priest my homily
would be,
mavericks/minorities
we're Canaanites, we heard the rumours
there is always good wine in Cana and not just
at weddings.
We ask for faith and wine.
Demons have become technicalities.

– *Matthew* 15: 21–25

To be like me you must look at your hunger
and see it. If you like life, life with good things,
you will not find life. For what can stretching
your years do if you can not receive ideas?
We are orchards, if you stick around you can
manage to hang as good fruit, that is a saint.
The figure of God – justice love mercy images –
will come to interview us: the angels, beside him
and behind him, will carry in gifts and presents.

– *Matthew* 16:25–27

"No one has gone back up except the one who
descended – Me, Man's
Son. So as Moses swayed the reptile, so I am held up
so people can see life.

God got so excited about the world he sent his Son to
cavort in it so that
everyone on the dance floor might hear endless music.
God did not send his
Son into the world with a sour face but that they might
find the dancing master".

– *John* 3:13–17

Should you care whether you're first or last. Last best
bet.

"I am not free to do as I wish with my money?"
sounds like
a Libertarian text; it's a slot in the Gospel where you
have
to wonder was the scribe drinking?

Or maybe the tax-collector author was having a bad
day
but that's alright as Jesus ends by saying the
unqualified
may get into heaven before the qualified.

– *Matthew* 20:15–16

I will not and I did. The roadfork from rebellion to clarity. I did, I went out into the vine heat. Give starvation wine. One grape a time. Preferably one should talk only to one high priest and youngsters. Others went into the yard: tax collectors for the community budget, and prostitutes to set up some idea of love. There is no such thing as just an earthly love.

– *Matthew* 21:28–32

DOLLS ON THE FLOOR

Eric Adams

As I was writing this essay protests were erupting in Madison, Wisconsin, over union organizing rights. It is, in my mind, a worthwhile entry point in discussing James Liddy, his personality, poetry and ultimately his religiousness. He would have taken a ferocious interest in this political story and it would have become a significant part of the programme of many a night's discussion. James was politically and morally aligned with the labour movement, but he would have violently dismissed most of the rhetoric that comes with it. He was against the rich, but not the elite. He was for the poor, but not against poverty. And any notion of protecting a middle-class family would have been grudgingly tolerated as an evil means toward a good end.

The protests, which have turned me into as much of a news junkie as James had been, seem meaningful in that they provide parenthesis to the time since James passed. Anyone familiar with the Irish demeanor might already have guessed his affection for political moments. I was visiting James at the now defunct Columbia Hospital across the street from UWM with a group of friends composed mostly of his ex-students. It had become a bit of a routine for a week or so to finish teaching and then stop for a chat as he was being prepared for treatment. James was passionately supportive of Obama and so I stayed to watch the returns. He was not as engaged as I expected and, in retrospect, I can see he was disengaging with this world. He smiled and nodded as someone who was trying to please the enthusiasm of another. Eventually he grew tired and I left to meet friends at bar-bowling alley to watch the returns even though I needed to teach in the morning. I got the call as I was walking in my door. The consensus from that time was that we, the people who knew him, were glad he got to see what we all thought was an important moment and knew it would have been a terrible shame for him to miss. In the hospital the doctors were in awe of James' acceptance of the immediateness of his situation. He was, of course, communing with them in 75% poetical wit, as he did with most people.

It's been marked thoroughly that James lived poetry and history in his day-to-day life. His poetry is marked by a regular conversational ebb of people, places and moments. "Write about some *thing*", he would say to his students, not as advice, but in annoyance with the youthful desire to harness the abstract. The roots of so many of his poems are in the actual (or imagined) statements of real people. He looked beyond the meaning of people's language to their possible poetic truths. He unearthed and made real so many figures of the arts for his students, most notably Lorine Niedecker. His teaching style was simple: read, write and talk. Of course, his talk was inspired by the fact that these were real people with real gossip surrounding them. He led several pilgrimages of writing students, both graduate and undergraduate, to Niedecker's "condensory" on Black Hawk Island. One value of the poet with local roots was the ability to illustrate the real things of her life. The shack in which she lived with her deaf mother is no bigger than most backyard sheds. The place still floods every spring. Her grave in a nearby cemetery is only a few rows from the grave of her father's other family, including the grave of his daughter also named

Lorine. And he took students to Club 26, a supper-club she wrote of having a grasshopper in. He bought, but with alcohol only.

Yeats also had a particular importance for James and it was two poems, "The Magi" and "The Dolls", that became touchstones in discussions I had with him. I had focused on them in an essay exam for a Yeats class he taught at UWM. I don't remember or have a record of those responses, but they must have been fixed on an interpretation of the world as a horrible, beautiful place. "The uncontrollable mystery on the bestial floor" is the last line of "The Magi" and it became a part of our language when discussing the "real" world, encompassing both the stable floor on which Jesus was born and the barbaric world in which we live. In "The Dolls" enraged dolls in a doll-maker's house point at a cradle and say, "The man and the woman bring/ Hither, to our disgrace,/A noisy and filthy thing". The sentiment toward the world is again clear, but James always sneered at this. "I like babies", he would say defiantly. He liked them crying in churches and restaurants. "They should be brought into the bar. That's the real thing".

James thrived in the contact zone of contradiction. It occurred to me as I used the poems of William Blake in my Western Civ. Lit. class, that in contradiction there must be some quintessential value for the human mind – not in the form of a knowledge, but the performance it demands. The exploration of Christianity that Blake creates in the juxtaposition of "The Lamb" and "The Tyger" pushes the mind beyond easily reasoned answers. And this is where I find myself thinking about the intersection of James' religiousness and character.

I should describe his religiousness as a dual entity. He certainly had and expressed a belief in God, but he also had a love of the Roman Catholic Church. This love was a real sort of love – jealous, vulnerable, and inspired. People who knew him may immediately recognize this description of love as it seemed to permeate his relationships with all things on this "bestial floor". The church for him is in the place between the "bestial floor" and heaven. He had a strong partisan relationship to it as with any other topic. To be in his presence, which was to be in the centre of conversation, one always risked saying something that might make him leap in his chair. He would shred conventional interpretations of anything, particularly good Catholicism or notions of love. He would defend the church in the same tiger-daddy way. James was a revolutionary Catholic, as far as I understood it, not in the popular form. He was opposed to liberation theology because it seemed to rely too much on the destruction of the elite ideas of culture. The poetry of Christ lies in the things he says to destroy what exists too easily. James emphasized this in the way he talked about everything, through a lens of the world too corrupt and too blessed to be taken for granted.

For me, and probably many of his other students, he was an introduction to just about everything. James often referred to me as a Scottish rationalist. He liked to highlight ethnic information in his understandings of people's character. The only topic of which I knew less than poetry when I met James was religion. My mother and I have a strange parallel, in that we were both raised in very secular families and our first significant encounter with religion came in the form of Southern Baptists. They came around our suburbs – her's Detroit, mine Madison – picking up children in big blue buses and taking them on excursions: to the mall, the baseball game, or to their rural retreats. James interjected when I first told him this story, "You met your people". My mother and I both realized that we distrusted organized religion, I much quicker than she. So a few years later in my second childhood, I met an Irish Catholic and (politely) declared my so-called atheism. And that poet said, "Of course, you're Scottish", and directed me to read the poems and autobiography of Edwin Muir. The way he made all of these things "real" to me also made me think much more reasonably about them.

– March 2011

About the Author

James Liddy was born in Lr. Pembroke St., Dublin, in 1934. His parents hailed from the cities of Limerick and New York. He lived in Coolgreany, County Wexford, intermittently from 1941 to 2000. His books include *In a Blue Smoke* (Dolmen, 1964), *Blue Mountain* (Dolmen, 1968), *A Munster Song of Love and War* (White Rabbit, 1971), *Baudelaire's Bar Flowers* (Capra/White Rabbit, 1975), *Corca Bascinn* (Dolmen, 1977), *Collected Poems* (Creighton University Press, 1994), *Gold Set Dancing* (Salmon, 2000), *I Only Know that I Love Strength in My Friends and Greatness* (Arlen House, 2003), *On the Raft with Fr. Roseliep* (Arlen House, 2006), *Wexford and Arcady* (Arlen House, 2008), *The Askeaton Sequence* (Arlen House, 2008), *Fest City* (Arlen House, 2010) and *It Swings from Side to Side* (Arlen House, 2011).

He was a Professor in the English Department at the University of Wisconsin-Milwaukee for many years, where he taught creative writing and Irish and Beat literature. *James Liddy: A Critical Study* by Brian Arkins was published by Arlen House in 2001 and the widely acclaimed *Honeysuckle, Honeyjuice: A Tribute to James Liddy*, edited by Michael S. Begnal, appeared in 2006.

The first volume of his memoir, *The Doctor's House: An Autobiography* was published by Salmon in 2004, with volume two, *The Full Shilling*, appearing in 2009.

This is the final collection James was working on before he passed away on 5 November 2008 following a short illness. A selected volume is in development.